"Gunilla Norris brings a new awareness
of the sacred nature of all life."
–ANNE BANCROFT, author of *Weavers of Wisdom*

"Gunilla Norris doesn't tell you what to see, but
how to see. She doesn't tell you where to go, but
how to know when you have arrived."
–RABBI RAMI SHAPIRO

"Gunilla Norris's meditations
are beautiful and human
and show the glory in the ordinary."
–MADELINE L'ENGLE

"Gunilla Norris's remarkable reflections
on friendship inspire and guide us to the deep
place where we can 'see the stars in one another.'"
–JOYCE RUPP, award-winning author

"Just reading [Norris'] makes you want to
sit down, take a deep relaxing breath,
and refresh your spirit."
–JACK KORNFIELD, author *A Path with Heart*

Touched
by Blessing

GUNILLA NORRIS

Guilla Norris

LITTLE BOUND BOOKS
WWW.LITTLEBOUNDBOOKS.COM

LITTLE BOUND BOOKS

WWW.LITTLEBOUNDBOOKS.COM

All Rights Reserved
Published in 2020 by Homebound Publications
Cover & Interior Designed by Leslie M. Browning
Cover Illustration: © by KrisArt

ISBN 9781947003651
First Edition Trade Paperback

10 9 8 7 6 5 4 3 2 1

On the Wing

Joy is the Thinnest Layer

Match

Embracing the Seasons

Sheltered in the Heart

Being Home

Becoming Bread

Simple Ways

A Mystic Garden

Inviting Silence

Companion on the Way

Great Love in Little Ways

To my beloved grandchildren

Chloe

Hannah

Jacob

Naomi

Riley

Acknowledgments

Many thanks to my editor Leslie Browning
or her trust in my work.

Gratitude to Natalie Billing for her careful
reading and wonderful suggestions.

And love to dear friends who read
the manuscript at different stages
and gave me support.

Table of Contents

An Introduction to Blessing and Mutual Reflection

I once lived in a house with a small living room. The room had windows on only one wall, so it tended to be a dark space that felt tight and enclosed. When mirrors were strategically placed in two corners and on one other wall, the room suddenly became alive with light and felt much larger. Due to the reflecting mirrors, the light and spaciousness of the out-of-doors filled the room. It became a cozy, warm place to be.

When I think about the transformation of that room, I see it as a metaphor about mutual reflection. Whenever we mirror the light and goodness of another person, our common *living room* expands and is illumined. This is profound work that anyone can do. In times that are dark and difficult, we can feel both helpless as well as enraged and flip between the two states. What can sustain us? What can we be *for* without feeling ambivalent? I think it is the capacity to bless. The more we bless the more blessing there is. As abundant as salt is in the ocean, so blessing can be in our lives. When we understand this, we will find the amazing secret that in blessing we are in turn blessed.

We all have chances to transform what is confining and dark. A blessing may at first be experienced as very daunting: a diagnosis we dread, the loss of a loved one, a sudden change we are not prepared for. Yet, it is in meeting these *challenges* at our door that we might also meet what can make us whole. At the core, blessing is a way of claiming that even though goodness might for a time be invisible, it is nevertheless as close to us as breathing.

Blessing is always relational. As we reflect and act to support the goodness we see in others, we enhance one another and bring light to whatever we may be experiencing. We will be serving *Life* itself, and in doing so, much can change. Every single day, we can engage in small acts of mutual reflection and consideration that enlarge our common living spaces with possibility and goodness. This is immensely powerful. No such actions will ever be lost, though we may never see their ultimate outcomes.

To be seen, witnessed, and reflected touches us deeply. To be deeply touched, in a way that aligns with our nature, desire, or need is to be confirmed. This little book is about the blessing that arises out of such mutual recognition and reflection. I will tell you four stories that happened to me. They transformed me. Like reflecting mirrors, they brought more light into the paths my life has taken. Though the stories may not seem at first to belong to each other, they contain a similar message. In each one, I was blessed by what transpired. I hope these stories will inspire you to both mirror and reflect the light in others, and to remember your own blessing stories, particularly the ones that opened you, confirmed you, and helped to further your life.

I love little books like this, and I hope you do, too. Though they are quickly read, they can remind you, the reader, of something that feels like a necessity, something you need to mull over, digest, and put into use. I hope this will be true for you in reading this little book. To share our experiences, and to find joy in them brings us mutual light, inspiration, and confirmation.

Notes About Blessing

God bless you, we say when someone sneezes. Once long ago, it was thought that when someone sneezed, their soul left their body, and so a blessing was needed to bring the soul back home. We don't think this way in our time, but there is nevertheless an intuitive knowing that the soul needs blessing and a safe home within the consciousness of our being. This continues to be true.

In English, the word *blessing* comes from the old English word *bloedsing*, whose meaning was to sanctify and consecrate with blood.

I know that sounds gory! However, ancient people held blood to be a symbol for life. So to join one's blood, that is, one's life force, and to commit one's self to another person's well being, was a powerful vow of mutuality.

Even now, in Sweden, where I come from, it is still the custom whenever we make a promise we intend to fulfill to "thumb on it". *Vi tummar på det*, we say. With this little ritual act of commitment, one's promise is no longer casual. This custom is left over from times when we would cut our thumb so it would bleed, and one's friend would do the same. In the mingling of blood was placed a promise, a vow of constancy, an offering of self. Even now, in some places in the world people become *blood brothers* and *blood sisters* in this way.

These customs reflect that blessing is a prayer that invokes the life force to be with those we bless. When we recognize that something has blessed us, we sense how the life force has somehow given us the strength to live more fully.

Blessing is a heart-full practice. The heart pumps blood, and the blood circulates to every part of the body. We are constantly infused by the flow of blessing from our physical heart. When we bless others and are blessed by others, we are also circulating energy, support, and the wish for one another's best interests. Our hearts are in it.

A received blessing always takes place in the here and now, in a specific time and place. It is usually on the edge of the unknown and meets the need of a moment. It is also true that blessing is *in the air* all the time, though we might not have a practice of invoking it or feeling it.

To live in the awareness of blessing is to practice a very human art that sanctifies the simplest of things. For instance, blessing our food before we eat it brings about deeper nourishment. Turning on the light when it's dark, understood as a blessing, sheds more light than what electricity delivers. Opening the faucet and feeling clean water run over our hands or drinking a cup of clear water is to wash and drink blessing. Without water we cannot live. Opening the window and breathing the morning air will inspire us with more than we know. Holding the hand of your child, a friend's hand, or the hand of a spouse or a stranger...even perhaps the hand of an enemy... will keep our hearts open to blessing.

I love the African aphorism that Bishop Desmond Tutu often shared: *"I am because we are"*. It tells the truth that mutuality is at the core of life. We cannot do without each other. The Swedish Nobel Prize winner for poetry, Tomas Tranströmer wrote in a poem (and I loosely translate here), "We are that place where Life is working on itself". We need each other's reflection to do it, to bring illumination into each other's living spaces.

We are made whole by each other's loving presence and being. To become aware of this, even just a little, is to participate in miracles. Blessings that reach into our hearts and those that emerge from our hearts make a force for goodness that does not quit.

To end this note I want to include what the Sufi poet, Hafiz, wrote. It speaks of a spiritual mutuality that is astonishing. If what he wrote is true, we have the possibility to live in a radiance of such enormity it cannot be imagined.

"God revealed a sublime truth
to the world
when He sang,
I am made whole by your life.
Each soul, each soul completes me."

Becoming a
Pennacook

I

Dreaming in the Dark

This story begins when I was seven or eight. At the time I lived in Sweden and would visit my grandparents on school holidays with siblings and cousins. I remember that it took a long time to travel to the remote place where they lived. First there was the long train ride departing from Stockholm and arriving at the little hamlet of Sveg, in the district of Härjedalen, above the Arctic Circle. Disembarking from the train, we were tucked into a sled with warm stones and piles of bear pelts and woolen blankets to keep us warm.

The road was hard-packed with snow, at least a meter thick. As the horse pulled our sled, we rocked back and forth in our warm cocoon past miles of tall pines. We were surrounded by deep stillness. The only sound was the creak of the sled and the footfall of the horse as it moved deeper into the landscape. We loved this trip to the remote village of Lofsdalen. In that hamlet there were no electric lights, no telephones, and no indoor plumbing. In the winter, there was early darkness. Stars were visible as early as three in the afternoon. Sometimes at night we could hear owls or an occasional wolf calling in the stillness.

After a long time in the sled, it was heaven to arrive and to be folded into our grandparent's log cabin at the foot of a mountain called Hoverken. There, in the high plateau country near the Norwegian border was snow...endless snow... snow...snow. During the day, we would put on our long, narrow, Lapp skis and exhaust ourselves skiing for hours on the plowed road or down the nearby hills. By late afternoon our skis would stick up like porcupine quills in the heaped snow banks near the entrance of the cabin. Our cheeks were bright red and chapped, even though we had bear grease or Nivea cream rubbed into them before we ever went outside.

Dinner was often the simple fare of the north–cheese, hard tack, herring, potatoes and occasional eggs. Tuckered out as we were, we retired early to our bedroom. It was a room with a table, a chair, an oil lamp, and a chamber pot (since going to the outhouse in the cold, especially when it was snowing, was considered dangerous). Built into the far wall were six bunk beds: two-side by-side sets of three beds stacked on top of each other. The combination of our warm breaths and a corner fire kept the room temperature above freezing.

Now, after dinner, and after crawling under the covers, came my favorite time of the day. Grandmother took a seat by the wide wooden table in the bedroom. She lit an oil lamp, opened a book, and read out loud to us. We were safe, warm, and transported into stories that opened our minds to worlds far away. We heard fairy tales and classics. One of the books Grandmother read was James Fennimore Cooper's novel, *The Last of the Mohicans*, translated into Swedish.

Aaah! That story planted a seed in my young heart. Oh, to be a native! To live and to be completely at home in the wilds was a dream. To be brave and honorable and to overcome whatever difficulties I would encounter, that was something to admire!! I wanted to be THAT! Tucked under several blankets in the depth of the dark winter, I was imagining being a Mohican. It wasn't the least bit clear to me what that really meant, but it called my spirit deeply.

II
Seedlings

I first came to the United States when I was nine years old. We lived in New Rochelle, N.Y., while my father, a Swedish diplomat, worked at the consulate in New York City. I was to enter third grade, and one way or another, I was to learn English. There was no choice about that, or about learning to fit in.

To learn English, Mother and Father refused to speak to us in Swedish. It was like learning to swim by being thrown into deep water. This was at a time when television was just beginning to be in people's homes. How extraordinary TV was to us! Our family did not have a television, so my siblings and I would go next door to watch *Howdy Doody* and *Tom Mix*. The latter was my favorite, of course. There on the screen were *my* Indians. I loved seeing them ride over the plains, brave and fearless. They were my icons. With everything so new and strange to me, I needed very much to be fearless.

There was a little stand of trees in our backyard. It was my very own forest, and in it I built my tepee, made my bows and arrows, and pretended to be the Indian I imagined. I still remember the smell of the earth and the feeling of possessiveness I had for my camp. Somehow I learned English along the way. But that was not as important to me. What was important was that the seed, planted in the far North, had taken silent root in my young being.

III

Kachina Wisdom

My life took twists and turns. As a pre-teen I found myself living in Houston, Texas, where my father had been commissioned to establish a consulate for the South West area of the United States.

Why Houston? It's the third-largest port in the country. Much trade happens there from all over the world.

Adjusting to life in the South was not easy for me. The humidity and the heat alone were suffocating. It was as if a large, wet, blanket of wool was smothering me. Also, the sweet Southern words, *Y'all come,* which might seem welcoming on the surface, often turned out not to be sweet at all. Below the surface were other meanings, and they were confusing and a bit scary. I was different from my classmates. I knew they talked about me behind my back because I didn't wear makeup or moon over boys. I didn't have the latest version of the *in* clothes that were popular. Many times my phone calls were not returned. Invitations seemed based on social status or some other criterion. I was not mature enough to understand social deception. My guard was up. I didn't know whom to trust.

One blistering summer, my sister and I were sent away to a camp called Cimmaroncita in New Mexico. We needed relief from the heat.

I knew the state was full of tribal territories. That was exciting indeed! I don't remember how we traveled there, but I remember the huge, blue, New Mexican sky opening above me, the Sangre de Christo Mountains rising in front of me, and I was transported. For me it was a first glimpse into how small human beings actually are. I began to see that we live in an immensity beyond comprehension. Compared with what had seemed to be fake sweetness in the *y'all come,* this landscape was truthful and an antidote for me. It gave me a feeling of trust and freedom.

Later in the summer I saw my first Kachina doll. The gooseflesh rose on my arms. In some inexplicable way, I already knew something about them. Even then I could sense that these dolls represented spirits and aspects of the natural world: the sun, stars, thunderstorms, wind, corn, and many other things. Only later did I learn that Kachinas are viewed as powerful beings. If given veneration and respect, they use their powers for human good, bringing much-needed rainfall, healing, fertility, or protection. I was beginning to understand that life and meaning were all around me, especially in nature.

At the time I didn't understand much of this. All I knew was that something had awakened in me. Why did this all seem so important, strange, and yet familiar? The little seed planted long ago when I was much younger was sprouting, and unbeknownst to me, was secretly growing.

IV
Serving Life

Stories do not always unfold sequentially. There are detours and interruptions. My life continued to unfold. I grew up, married, and had two children. At twenty-six, I found myself living in a little town next door to West Point, New York, along the banks of the Hudson River. Our two small children were four and three. We loved being by the river and feeling, even as far away from the sea as we were, the river's tidal flow. In the autumn, when the river was warmer than the air, lacey wafts of white steam rose from it. And every month the full moon shimmered in the running water. I loved sitting on the veranda watching the *river-being* as it made its way to the sea.

Our town was small and was bordered by the Hudson on one side, and by Bear Mountain and West Point on two other sides. In the past, West Point had what was called "The Black Cavalry". Members of that cavalry brought their families up from the south to live in our little town of Highland Falls. This was still true at the time we lived there. Not only African Americans, but also Latin Americans, were in that group, and they, too, brought their families into town. Often these family members lived below the radar of social services.

Over time it came to my attention that quite a few hidden youngsters were in town. These kids were unprepared for kindergarten. I felt bad for them. Through no fault of their own, they were not getting what they needed. And so I was inspired to start a little school to remedy that situation and began to work towards making it happen.

It didn't take long for *The Get Set School* to come into being...a miracle of co-operation and many willing hands. $4,000.00 dollars was raised to pay the head teacher's salary. The nearby Catholic college provided student teachers who were given credit toward their degrees. Doctors and dentists in town gave the kids services for free. For some children this was the first time they had ever seen a doctor. The hardware store provided playground equipment and much more. Here was a town that was taking care of its own!

To find and register the kids for school, I had to go into homes where too many people were living illegally and in crowded conditions. I remember one living room where I was hoping to register a couple of Latin American toddlers. My Spanish was rusty to say the least. As I acted out mumps and chickenpox and other diseases that I didn't have the Spanish names for, the room filled with more and more people grinning and laughing at me. Before I was done, I think there were thirty warm bodies in a tiny 10 + 12 room. I now believe that the comedy of my plight to register the children allowed those mothers and fathers to feel a sense of safety. The word spread that our little school might be an okay place to send their children. In the end, to my delight, we had more than fifteen students enrolled.

As it happened, there was an annual Native American gathering along the banks of the Hudson River. In the fall, tribes from Florida and all the way from Canada were represented. To raise awareness and support for the issues that the Native American population had, their leaders selected three candidates to be initiated as members of one or another of the tribes. They chose people whom they thought were ones that had contributed significantly to the community. In this way, newspapers would cover the story and bring attention to the often forgotten needs of the Native American community

To my astonishment I was chosen because of *The Get Set School*. I was thrilled. My wish to become an Indian was being granted! I could hardly believe this would be so. It struck me as somehow right that I would be a Native American first, before I ever became an American citizen, which took place years later.

On the day of the initiation I went to the gathering with my family. We walked among the open fires. We ate grilled rattlesnake (it tastes a bit like grilled chicken). We sampled acorn bread laced with maple syrup. We saw beautiful beadwork being done and heard the steady beat of drums. I couldn't help but remember my makeshift tepee in the backyard in New Rochelle. Knowing what was about to happen this day, the little kid I was back then would have been over the moon.

At last it was time to assemble for the ceremony. The sound of rattles filled the air. Drums pounded. Presiding, Chief Red Tomahawk stepped out on the makeshift stage. He wore glorious regalia and a headdress with horns. Spirits were called from the four directions. The two congressmen who were also being honored were summoned to the front of the room. In a very realistic depiction, the chief placed his tomahawk against the necks of the congressmen. "The white man" had to be symbolically killed before they could be initiated. After his ritual death, each man was assigned a tribe and a native name.

During the ceremony, I glanced at my children and saw that their eyes were enormous and full of anxiety. I could do nothing about it for I was up next. When called to the front, I was placed next to Princess Heather Flower of the Montauk. The drums softened. Chief Red Tomahawk, who seemed immense to me in his finery, took my right arm and turned it up so that my veins would be exposed. He did the same with Princess Heather Flower's wrist. He placed my wrist over hers and laid a leather strap over both our arms.

The drums stopped beating. For a moment everything was silent. The Chief looked penetratingly into my eyes. Never before had I been seen and recognized in this way. Slowly he spoke and said, *"Nothing in you needs to be killed. Women serve life."* Then with a deep and resonating voice, he commissioned me to, *"Serve Life."* Those commanding words reverberated in me. They penetrated to my core. I was thrumming and knew I had received a profound blessing as well as my marching orders. At the end of the ritual he also gave me my native name, *Nippe*, Algonquin for clear water.

What happened next took my breath away. The chief assigned me to the Pennacook tribe in Northern New England. I was astonished!

My husband and I had summered there, in Pennacook land, for years! How did the Chief intuit this? How, knowing nothing about me, had he somehow put me squarely where we already had a little cabin in the woods? I will never know. It would remain a mystery. But he sensed to which tribe I was to be assigned. From that moment, I would always know that I had been seen and instructed as well as named and blessed...a gift I am still receiving.

Now, whenever I am confused and need direction or guidance, I ask, "What will serve *life* here?" It's not what will serve me, or others I love, or ones I might be in conflict with. To sense what will serve life itself, and then to act on it, seems never to be wrong. The question has not failed me yet. I offer it to readers and friends to use whenever they need a way to cut through what is difficult or confusing.

What I learned in the odd twists and turns of my journey is that what really belongs to any one of us cannot be kept from us, even though years may separate events. Life circumstances may look as if they are random. They are not. Hints are often there in our early years. Something touches us and somehow awakens a truth we are to live into. For me, the wish "to be a Mohican" would, in time, develop in ways I could never have guessed.

When we listen deeply we can find organic ways to respect the life force that is inherent in everything. There is always a hidden confluence in what is transpiring. Many things must converge and everything isn't up to us. Life knows where it is going, even if we don't. We are just a little part. But being small, and seemingly insignificant in the vastness of reality, is not a diminishment. It's simply the truth. Wherever we might be, we can somehow serve *Life* itself.

Mutual Radiance

I

A Stark Time

After twenty-eight years of marriage, I was sadly divorced, living alone in an old farmhouse in Connecticut while trying to start a brand new life. I was emotionally shaken by the break up. My husband had been unwilling to work on repairing our relationship. We had come to a place where the trust between us was no longer there. Perhaps, in fact, we had outgrown each other. We were no longer good for each other.

For me it was a stark time. I felt I needed a radical change of perspective. So I did the classical thing and decided to go on a trip as far away from what was familiar to me as possible. I knew I needed distance to be able to discern where I was, and where I needed to focus my attention to make important changes that could lead to a whole new way of life.

A good friend was taking a group of women to Bali. So I signed up. I paid for the trip even though I couldn't really afford it at the time, and packed my bag. It was a long flight with a lay over in San Francisco, then sixteen or more hours to Bali. When the plane door opened, the heat bowled me over. It was like a wall of humid fire. That impact made me instantly realize that I was not only far away from home, but that I was about to be plunged into experiences that would surely overwhelm me. Everything was *different*. It was exciting. And it was scary. Little did I know then how much I would be changed by what would happen to me in this very foreign country.

The group explored many things from batik making, silver-smithing, to shadow puppet shows, not to mention viewing Balinese dancing, holy rituals and more. These were exotic and wonderful experiences, but they are not the story I want to tell. The story that changed my life was about climbing Mt. Batur, the Father mountain of Bali.

After several days of exploring the artistic wealth in the Balinese culture, we set out in two small buses. We rode inland with two young men as our guides. The rice fields were beautiful, built in terraces up the hills. The road snaked through small villages with their central meeting spaces: large, open platforms covered by roofs, where village matters would be settled, as well as puppet shows given and festivals enjoyed. Dotting the landscape were resting places protected from the noonday heat. These were bamboo platforms with thatched roofs, raised high off the ground on wooden pillars. Whatever breeze could be felt would come up through the bamboo flooring. The low walls were simple barriers to keep children from falling off. Up there a breeze could easily be caught from east or west. We often saw families and friends resting and laughing together, enjoying their high perches through the worst heat of the day.

One thing in particular that I noticed and loved in Bali was how comfortable people were touching one another. It reminded me of my native Sweden, where girlfriends would hold hands going down the street. When I arrived in the U.S. at age nine in 1947 such a demonstration of affection between friends of the same sex was frowned upon, which saddened me.

In Bali, modesty is not easy to maintain. That took some getting used to! It came home to me particularly in one of the places we stayed. The bathrooms were open-air affairs. There were more than a few times when some mischievous children peered down at us over the privy's privacy wall. The kids tittered, pointed, and laughed at the American ladies relieving themselves. It was funny I admit.

The traditional homes in Bali are platforms raised a bit off the ground with roofs of bamboo and other indigenous materials. Generally they have two bearing walls and some sturdy posts to hold the roof in place, but one can pretty much see everything that is happening inside. I was told that a newly married couple would have only one night of privacy in a four walled dwelling. The rest of the time, all of life was led in the open so to speak. The main meal was prepared in the wee hours of the morning, around four, because it was cool enough then to have an open fire. All the leftovers were eaten during the day since refrigeration in traditional homes was rare at that time.

In the late afternoon we arrived at the modest, hostel-like hotel at the foot of the mountain. Lugging my things across the grass lawn to my simple room, I didn't see a large gaping hole. But my foot found it. I went down like a tree. My ankle twisted badly. Sprawled on the ground, my first thought was *so much for climbing Mt. Batur.*

My ankle swelled up into a glorious puffiness. Only with support from my friends, was I able to hobble back to the main building. There, we were met by *Made* (pronounced Mahdeh), the manager, cook, mountain guide, and village healer. At the time I didn't know he had all those responsibilities, or that he would change my life. To me he was simply a slender, attractive man wearing a sarong and a smile. My guess was that he was in his late twenties or early thirties.

I was given water and then *Made*, in his broken English, told me to lie down, which required another painful hobble back to my room. He advised me to elevate my leg. He offered to perform a healing for me after he was finished with cooking our dinner and the necessary clean up afterwards.

Lying down in my room, far away from the kind of medical help I was used to, I felt very vulnerable. I was scared. There I was on my back, on a pallet, in the middle of seeming nowhere with all its unfamiliar ways. I felt very alone and sorry for myself in more ways than one. The room seemed to shrink. I knew darkness would come soon and suddenly, the way it does near the equator. Foreign sounds filled the air. The whole sorry truth was there in the sheets with me. I was divorced. I was lonely. I hurt badly and I was shaking with fear.

The minutes crawled by. It seemed an eternity until it was time for supper. With help, I hobbled to the dining room, and we sat down to our meal. It was a modest affair. But we were glad to have it, as we were in a remote part of the country, away from city life and its many culinary offerings. I was just beginning to understand that this man who was serving us food was also serving in a much bigger way than we could possibly know.

Made means *three*. Balinese children at the time were named *one, two, three, four,* along with their family's last name. If there were a fifth child, it would be named *one,* starting all over again. Obedience to the will of the father was a very strong cultural rule. If a member of the family went against the father's wishes, that person would become an outcast. At that time, no other village would take them in. They would be shunned, something much feared in that culture. For a Westerner, this lack of individual freedom would be unthinkable. I would later come to appreciate something about this, which would not have been in my awareness otherwise.

After dinner *Made* offered to do a healing for my ankle. He asked me to sit down. I did, with friends surrounding me. He took my swollen ankle in his hands and began manipulating it. The pain was outrageous! I cried out loud. My friends were immediately afraid for me and told me I should not allow any more of what they thought would injure me. I don't know what let me trust *Made* in that moment. But I did. There was in his hands a kind of physical "knowing". The pain was dreadful, but I could feel gentleness in the way he was working with my ankle. I sensed he knew what he was doing, and so I allowed him to continue.

It's hard to remember physical pain when it's over, but this pain was not far from the remembered pain of childbirth. I cried. I yelped. I squirmed. I bit my lips. I howled. I held my breath. But I turned myself over to the pain, not thinking about what would come of the trust I was giving to *Made*.

The session lasted about an hour. Using borrowed crutches that were miraculously found for me, I got back to my room and fell into bed, exhausted. Full of worry, I wondered if *Made's* treatment had made things worse? Had I been foolish to allow it? The pain was still there. Would I be able to walk well enough to even get safely back home again?

My mind whirled. I knew we were to leave for the climb at 4:30 the next morning. The early start was due to the heat. We'd be up the mountain by mid morning if all went well. It was now nine at night, and I didn't think I would sleep, or that my ankle would be able to carry my weight in the near future. I was a trembling, sweaty rag far from home. Dark foreboding thoughts clung to me until sleep finally came.

II

Climbing Mount Batur

I woke at four. To my surprise I had slept deeply. Even this early in the morning the air was humid. My sheets were damp. I wiggled out of them and tried gingerly to move my injured ankle. It moved! Amazingly it moved without pain. I circled my foot to the left and to the right. I could see no swelling. I began to wonder if I dared go on the climb with the others. Bearing weight on the leg would be a test. So, I hung my legs off the pallet and stood up slowly. No pain. I put all my weight on the injured leg. No pain. Was this a miracle? Was it wise to stress the ankle and climb? I didn't think it was wise, but I wanted to go. Then and there I decided I was going to climb Mt.

Batur no matter what. I didn't realize then that I was gearing up to climb an inner mountain, the mountain of worry and fear for my future.

Dressing quickly, I joined my friends where we had agreed to meet. It was four thirty in the morning. The light was just breaking. And there was *Made* in his sarong kneeling in prayer, perhaps asking for our safety before he took us up the mountain. He picked a bouquet of marigolds that were growing nearby and offered them in his Balinese way to his God. Then he turned and looked at me with a conspiratorial smile. I wondered if he knew something that I didn't. But there wasn't much time to wonder, for we needed to start up the trail.

The beginning was easy. We took our time. Mount Batur is a volcanic mountain. We could see black humps of lava strewn over the mountainside with luscious, tropical growth peeking out of the valleys and fissures that were everywhere.

Not long after we had been on the trail, it became steep and conversation stopped. We needed our breath for climbing. My ankle was tender but not painful. I had a sense of something growing inside me. Was it a freedom from worry? Was it a little bit more courage? I didn't know what it was. I was just taking one step at a time climbing the mountain with my friends.

After an hour and a half of climbing, we stopped to rest and drink water. The sun was up. The heat was beginning to simmer. Our two original guides who were with us from the start plunked themselves down next to each other. One laid his head in the other's lap, laughing and jabbering. I noticed again the carefree physical way the Balinese had with each other. How easy and right this expression of friendship seemed to me.

After a while the trek continued. Our sweatbands were sopping. The vegetation grew sparse.

The black volcanic rock was more visible. By nine o'clock we were at the summit. The sky was incredibly blue, not a cloud in sight. The sun was brassy. We felt high having reached the top. Spontaneously we held hands and did a little jig together to celebrate. I was amazed that my ankle still didn't hurt. Though it was vague, I sensed that I had begun to climb through loss, through niggling fear, and through anger about my past. It was a summit moment.

After more water, food, and rest, it was time to head back before we were entirely baked. But going down was much harder than going up. My ankle began to swell again, and I felt an ache that was strangely deep. I would later call it a bone ache. That was for emotional reasons more than anything. I needed to descend the mountain and to descend into more acceptance of the loss of my marriage and all the changes that had happened because of it.

Suddenly *Made* was beside me. All during the climb up, he had been in front of the group and appeared to have no concern for any of us. He was simply leading the way. But now he offered me his arm. To be offered support without asking for it was entirely new to me. To have a need anticipated, noticed, and acted upon was an amazing experience. It had so rarely happened in my life, I hardly knew how to respond.

As it turned out, an exquisite dance down the mountain began. Each time I needed assistance, *Made* somehow knew it and offered his arm. If he sensed I could handle the next set of steps on my own, he withdrew his arm, but he never left my side. To this day, almost forty years later, I can still feel *Made's* gentle awareness and ready help as a great balm. I was *moved* down that mountain in more ways than one.

When we reached the bottom, I was so filled with gratitude and could only think to offer *Made* some money for his kindness. I reached into my pocket to hand him money, when he took a quick step back, stood up straight, and with utter dignity said in his broken English, *"No. I am good for you. You are good for me."*

And that was that. But it wasn't. I felt in my core that I had done something very wrong by offering *Made* money. At that moment, I did not have a clue what that could be. I had just wanted to say thank you. But I sensed, in that gesture, that I had diminished him. He was not a servant to be paid and forgotten.

We departed from Mount Batur after a noonday meal, but a subtle shame continued to linger inside me. It was much later that I realized that *Made* had completely given of himself, no holds barred, and that by offering money I had not received his gifts from the level they had been given. Such straight out care at the healing session the night before and then the careful atten-*dance*

down the mountain were heart gifts. I had be-
smirched those gifts by my offer of money, and
I felt ashamed. To this day, I still feel remorse
about it.

What I didn't understand until many years
later was that I had been good for *Made*, too. My
trust in his gifts of care, and my receiving of
them, were my gifts to him. Perhaps when you
are number three with little chance to be treated
as an individual in your own right as is the custom in your culture, then, when a foreign woman
sees you as a valuable individual, trusts you with
her body, and receives your gifts fully, she is good
for you. By offering money to *Made*, I had put myself down without knowing it.

The truth was that *Made* and I had both given
and received a heart exchange. I like to call that
mutual radiance. Mutual radiance happens when
the usual habits of assessment and judgment are
absent and there is enough trust for things to

unfold organically. It is never planned. Mutual radiance happens in surprising and timely ways. Something of deep goodness is exchanged and felt between two people. They feel and honor each other's essence and uniqueness.

Since I had been in a situation for some years where I was not good for my husband, and he was not good for me, this experience with *Made* was new territory for me. It showed me that even being strangers, without a common language, there can still be a gracious mutual receiving, mutual giving, and mutual awareness.

III

Magic Happens

My Bali trip came to an end, but this story didn't end there. I flew back to my home in Connecticut. A day after arriving, I decided to attend a meditation session held by a group of friends I often practiced with. A day of meditation would be good for me I thought, and would help me return to my circumstances and give me a chance to be quiet and integrate some of what had happened to me on the trip.

We spent the day in silence. It was a good day of quiet. I felt more whole inside. But having sat so many hours in airplanes and now several hours on a cushion, my back was not happy. I was aching in fact. The retreat day ended. We were saying our goodbyes to one another when one of the younger men in the group, about the same age as *Made*, noticed that I was in pain and that my back was not quite right. It would be something this man would notice since he was a skilled chiropractor.

"Come here, Gunilla," he said gently. *"I want to give you a hug."*

So I came to him, and he folded me tightly into his arms. With my body steadied in this way, his skillful fingers adjusted my back. I heard my vertebrae crack and click into place from the bottom up. The sensation and the sound made me laugh out loud.

"Oh, thank you," I said feeling the relief.

Then I heard my friend say these words. *"I am good for you, and you are good for me."*

A chill came over my body. My hair stood on end. Tears came to my eyes. My breath faltered. Here were the very same words *Made* had spoken.

The synchronicity stunned me. From one end of the world to the other, I had again been given a message and a direction for my life. Space and time were eliminated. These words were to be my new beginning. I would try to live them fully. Now I understood. At any moment, any one of us has the possibility to give and receive from the heart. It's like turning on floodlights. When we see each other as gifts, there will always be goodness exchanged. It can be as small as a smile, a thank you, the opening of a door, or an offer to help. Whenever there is a conscious, noticing, presence that is not evaluating, but is simply appreciating with heartfelt kindness, *magic happens.*

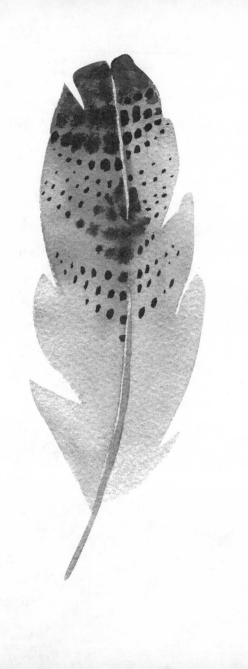

When the Veil Grows Thin

I

The Spirit of Animals

The lessons I learned in "Becoming a Pennacook" and in "Mutual Radiance" came mysteriously together in the next few years. It was the late 1980s. I was living in my old, Connecticut farmhouse. I needed not only to learn how to live as a single person, but also to make a steady income. Work became both focus and solace. Each week I did many hours of counseling. On the weekends I offered workshops and whole days of meditation retreats. It was also then that I began to write a book called *Being Home*. I knew how very much I needed to center myself and be home.

Having a sense of direction and purpose helped me to move on from my divorce and former life. The workload I assigned myself, however, was very tiring. I needed time off to replenish. The Episcopal Monastery of Holy Cross in West Park, New York was a place I would go for restoration.

The mighty Hudson River flows past the monastery. When I took time to be there, a sense of continuity with the river and with my Native American initiation along its banks returned. I believed I was "serving Life" in my work, but I was neglecting the serving of Life in myself. Those days along the river helped so much. It felt wonderful to traipse down the steep hill to the river's edge and to sense its flow to the ocean and back again. To me the river seemed to be breathing in long tidal breaths.

All along its shores I'd find wonderful skipping stones...flat, black pieces of shale. I skipped a great many of those stones into the water. They were my *wishing* stones, though I didn't really know what I was wishing for. Then came a turning point.

The 100th Jubilee of Holy Cross Monastery rolled around. Wanting to contribute something, I offered to bring seven large, felt banners I had sewn years before when I had suffered a long period of severe writer's block. During that time, I felt I had much inside me that I couldn't articulate. I was stymied. For me, writer's block was very painful.

So I took up sewing and made a huge, wordless book, six feet by eight feet, depicting stages in the spiritual journey. It took four years to finish, and I ruined at least one sewing machine in the process. I loved, however, that once the book was made and opened, and the banners hung, they made a room...something one could be inside of. For me, I always hoped that my writing would lead a reader to explore what was inside of them and find something they valued there.

I was very pleased when the banners were accepted for display. Since they were so huge, it was physically awkward to bring them to the monastery. But I was excited that finally people would see them. Storing them away had always felt sad.

I managed to lug the banners to Holy Cross, and I was fortunate to get help to hang the panels in the undercroft. It took some time, but once they were up, I felt very pleased and did a little jig in their presence, hoping no one saw me do it.

The next day the jubilee began. There was a festive service with many church dignitaries. There was a special meal in the dining room that overlooks the river. I wanted people to go to the undercroft and be pleased by what they saw. I secretly hoped they would say something affirming to me.

But the day passed. Not one person spoke to me. It was as if neither the banners nor I existed.

My happy expectations shriveled, and I spent a long, restless night tossing back and forth. In the morning I was determined to leave early, so I could go home and heal my disappointment as best I could.

I went to the undercroft to begin packing up. Then I saw something below one of the banners. It was a large, flat, river stone with a feather on top. What was this? The central image of the big book was a white swan maiden, an image I had chosen to represent the soul. Here was a white feather, perhaps a wordless form of recognition. Had someone seen and understood? Surely the feather was a message. Carefully I set the little offering aside, wanting to bring it home with me. As I struggled to roll up the banners, I heard footsteps. Turning around, I saw a young monk in a brown robe. He smiled and came into the room. Somehow I knew this was the person who had left me the offering.

I learned that his name was Lee Brunner. He was a Franciscan brother, living by special dispensation at Holy Cross, a house of Benedictine brothers. Now I understood the brown robe. Lee was tall and ruddy. He had high cheekbones. As we talked, I found out that his ancestry was mostly Cherokee. I also learned that his vocation was to offer spiritual dance as well as tai chi and chi gung classes at the monastery and in New York City.

What a huge help it was to have Lee's company while packing up. Slowly and a little shyly he told me that he had spent the whole night in the undercroft dancing with the images. I was touched. Here was the affirmation I had longed for. My book had meant something to someone.

"Lee, that means so much to me", I blurted and looked into his eyes in that soul-to-soul way that sometimes can happen. He gazed back. In that moment it felt as if we were in some other space

and time, and that we somehow knew each other from the inside out. Of course the moment broke after a little while. We laughed. Without having to say anything, we knew that we were connected in some way. What that connection would be was not clear, only *that it would be.*

Fortunately, I had friends in the Esopus and Woodstock N.Y. area near the monastery, so that going to Holy Cross for restoration was also a chance to visit my pals. Now with each visit to the area, Lee and I would also make time to be together. A connection grew, but not in any way I had experienced before. This was a friendship of an entirely different kind. We spent time in silence. We spent time apart. Yet there was always some deep and mysterious bond.

The friendship was sealed one afternoon when we walked together to the river's edge. Impulsively, and yet somehow also as if by command, we both jumped in. We were in the river up to our armpits, clothes and all, and began pouring water over each other. It was not a rambunctious game. It was more like a ritual of blessing, though not a single word was spoken. Later, we shook the river water off our clothes the way dogs do, and went our separate ways.

Trust and intuition became our language. It seemed that whenever I felt sad and lonely in my farmhouse, Lee would call on the phone. How did he know? Since calling a brother at the monastery was not done, I wrote letters to Lee. They arrived when they were needed. We didn't question this or talk about it. We were simply living it.

One day, when I was going home from visiting a pal in the Woodstock area, I passed the monastery. I felt a strong pull to turn around. I screeched to a halt as soon as I could and drove into the parking lot. Walking to the front door, and still not knowing why I had turned around, I glanced up and there was Lee in one of the Adirondack chairs on the lawn. He said he was waiting for me!

It was such a surprise. How did he know I was coming? Out of my mouth came these words, *"Lee, I think it's about the spirit of animals inside us. We need to find them."* Here was the essence of Kachina wisdom. Of course, I didn't really know what I was talking about, but Lee calmly answered. *"That must be why I canceled my trip to France."* Yes, he had been planning to travel, but canceled just hours earlier not knowing why. I could feel and trust that we would find out whatever it was that was calling us.

II
Small Steps

That very day we began to make plans to explore what we later called "our work". We knew that we were to intuit whatever animal presences seemed alive in the chakras or energy centers of our bodies. We agreed to spend a good deal of time both separately and together in silence, so as to allow our bodies to give us hints about this. We spent days trying to be fully present and to notice those hints. We only spoke during our simple meals. Silence, stillness, and intuition were the main ingredients of our process. Lee, a Franciscan, was more experienced than I was in contemplative practice, but I muddled along.

One morning I struggled with insistent and annoying *to do lists* crowding my thinking. I was outwardly silent but not still! Over and over I scanned my body to sense whatever I could, and it became apparent that I had a gnawing sensation in my solar plexus. Gnawing, gnawing.... It was uncomfortable. I hated that feeling. What animal was that inside me? It was unmistakable. A RAT. I was shocked. This was an ugly truth I didn't want to know. The next few hours I thought of hundreds of ways I could get rid of that rat. I was embarrassed and my self-image took a nosedive. I didn't want Lee to know.

After lunch that fateful day Lee and I took a walk in the neighborhood. We passed houses and a wood that was nearby. Suddenly, hurtling out of the trees, a rat bolted on to the pavement, ran over my feet and disappeared into a nearby culvert. I yelped and began shaking uncontrollably.

"Lee", I cried, *"I have a rat in my solar plexus. It's so awful and now I can't hide it. You saw one run over my feet. It's a confirmation. I feel so ashamed."*

Lee stood stock still in the street. That moment seemed like an excruciating time for me his opinion mattered so much to me. Slowly Lee smiled. *"I saw it, too."* he said. *"But don't you know, Gunilla, that it was the rat that first gnawed its way to the Buddha?"*

I gulped. I was still shaking. I heard the words, but it actually took many subsequent months to integrate the feeling of *ratness* in me. I knew that I couldn't help that feeling or get rid of it. I would persist in following a spiritual path no matter what, toward something I could sense, but could in no way describe. I was humbled and disgusted by the rat image. But, in truth, I was gnawing my way toward my heart's home.

Later, I began to understand that this rat encounter was a key. Could it be that every animal we discovered within ourselves would make a personal appearance in actuality? What was actuality anyway? Was a thinning between realms the experience we were to have?

I had a respect for nature and its creatures as never before. Could it be that in some small, incremental steps I was becoming more like an Indian? Was what my childhood-self had yearned for so long ago actually coming to be?

III

The Very Stuff of Life

Some of the animal spirits that Lee and I intuited as being inside us appeared outwardly when we were together. In particular, there was one memorable time when a friend gave us a house deep in the woods to use for a week. Going into the woods, whether actually or metaphysically, with only a vague feeling that you must go, is a classical metaphor for a spiritual journey.

Fasting had now become part of the process of our work. Several days before we set out together, we prepared separately. We gave up coffee and tea the first day, dense proteins like eggs and meat the second day. The third day we gave up carbohydrates such as rice and wheat. The fourth we gave up vegetables. The fifth day, with just fruit for our meals. We set off for our borrowed house. Ahead of us were many days of fasting, being in nature, and encountering whatever would surface either inwardly or outwardly.

We decided that we would spend our days in silence. Because Lee was a night person and I was a morning person, we designated a bowl in the hall to be our mailbox. In case either of us was in trouble we could leave a note in the bowl for the other.

Together we made a medicine wheel. We lugged 36 stones–the sacred number for such a circle–to a sunny glade that was close to the house. It was an act of preparation. We were ready to discover whatever we could and to live for a time without food, without goals, without expectations. *Nothing to do. No one to be. Nowhere to go.*

As the fast took hold, I found myself shivering. I piled on numerous sweaters. It was early fall. With each day a sense of greater vulnerability and lethargy came over me. I could make my way to the medicine wheel, sit inside it, and feel the earth hold me while my inner ground heaved and shook.

On the fifth day, I lay down in the sun on a little slope of land that overlooked the medicine wheel. I watched autumn leaves swivel and glow in the sunlight. Time seemed to be in suspension. A deep quiet had taken hold of me. This was not a *letting go*, but a simple *letting be*.

Then I saw Lee enter the medicine wheel. Soon after, a young buck was in the wheel with him. They began leaping, moving together as if they knew each other. I held my breath. I couldn't believe what I was seeing. Never before had I imagined such a thing. Here were two of God's creatures in deep accord and obvious joy. It was astounding to witness this leaping, moving, holy dance of mutuality.

Nearby a doe stood and watched as well. She was still. I was still. Every now and then her ears would swivel, and her eyes would gaze over at me. I wished I had ears that I could swivel. We watched until the dance came to a natural end. The buck and the doe melted into the trees. The only sound was that of rustling leaves. Lee lay down in the center of the medicine wheel filled with what I can only guess was as an immense sense of wonder. This event, beyond everything, sealed my knowing that mutual radiance is not only possible, but that it is the very stuff of life.

For me, fasting helped me to be more open. My self-protective tendencies took a back seat, and I could feel myself soften and be more trusting. Lee told me his experience with fasting was similar. Together we wondered if this feeling of ours was actually the absence of aggression. Could animals sense that we were not a threat to them? They could safely engage with us, and we with them. Lee and I felt deeply initiated by this. What had happened to him was an amazing instance of mutuality. And I was graced by something remarkable that I would never forget.

Some days later we returned to ordinary life. It was slow. We ate fruit the first day, vegetables the next, and so on in reverse of how we started our fast. We were eventually back, but we were also changed forever in a deep, tender, and inexplicable way.

IV

In the Eyes of a Humming Bird

Not every one of our animal encounters was this dramatic. For example, I found a bear in my base chakra, and subsequently I met the bear on a shore of Lake Nippising in Canada. I had been fasting as before. One day I was paddling a canoe and loving that my Algonquin name was *Nippe*. Dipping my paddle into the lake I could see how clear and cool the water was. *Nippe* on Nippising. I was having a sweet moment. When I looked up, I saw the bear. He was fishing with great concentration. Slowly and quietly I let the canoe glide toward the shore. The black bear looked up. It bared its teeth in what looked like a goofy smile. I smiled back baring my teeth in a similar grin.

With the paddle resting on the gunnel, the canoe slipped in closer. The bear paid me no mind. For me, it was more than enough to be that close. I stayed only a few minutes longer. No more was needed.

I did wonder, however, what Lee was encountering wherever he was. I learned later that he had, at about the same time, swum with a whale in California. It was yet another experience with one of the animals that belonged to him.

On that same trip to Canada I met my hummingbird, the animal of my crown chakra. I was sitting quite still in an Adirondack deck chair. The sun was warm and my fasting had brought me to a familiar quiet. Then the bird appeared, hovering at eye level. I could hear the *whirr* of its wings and feel the little breeze the wings created sweeping over my face. For a full five minutes the bird hung in the air before me...eye to eye. I did not need to interpret this in any way. It was sheer gift. To this day the hummingbird is for me the symbol of joy. Even now, decades later, I still see those little, dark eyes looking into my eyes. I can hear the wings, and my whole being deepens in reverence.

In time, Lee's and my "work" finished. Together and apart, we found every one of our animal energies. Each encounter was a gift we were fortunate to have. But the sense of radiance when the veil grows thin is what blessed us the most. I learned that it is possible to see things in a more than surface way, and that when we do that, we are graced to experience the underlying unity we are all part of.

Royal Guest

I

And Silence Began

Lee, my friend and soul brother, passed away. He was so young, only in his late thirties. It was wrenching to lose him and to lose the deep comfort of companionship in spiritual journeying. I was grateful for all we had experienced both together and apart. Our times in wilderness and silence changed my relationship to reality. But now, to not be *natives* in nature together anymore was hard to bear.

As a woman, it didn't feel safe to go into wilderness alone. Finding isolated natural settings and spending time there without the presence of another human being was not something I felt

I could handle. And fasting alone in such places could be truly dangerous.

Years went by. Was there anything I could do to satisfy my ongoing yearning to go deeper into the unknown? The rat was gnawing! Then from a friend I heard of the high hermitage at the Lama Foundation in New Mexico. Perhaps I could go there and be safe. Folks at the Foundation would know where I was. Yet I could be alone shedding the persistent and inhibiting layers of my ego. I wanted to experience again that open state of consciousness when the veil grows thin.

I booked my ticket to Santa Fe. Dear friends picked me up and drove me to the Lama Foundation. We arrived in a downpour. The rain was so insistent that the road melted into a river of red mud.

We thought we would wait out the rain, but it didn't stop. I was aware that my friends had else-where to go, so I decided to cover my head with a brown grocery bag and run to the office to meet the hermit master.

I was disappointed when I found she wasn't there. I was told to just unload my things in the kitchen, and to wait. Back I went into the rain. The brown bag, a bit torn by now, flapped around my head as if it had wings. Red mud splattered up my calves. Even though the weather was so inclement, I wanted to get on with my plans and release my friends to their destinations.

The rain made everything hasty and heavy. I hoisted my suitcase and sleeping bag out of the trunk. They seemed to have grown heavier than I remembered. Up the steep flight of stairs I went. Down again I came for the briefcase bulging with papers and books.

My friends gave me wet, farewell kisses. I watched them go and saw how the car slid in the mud and then slithered away. Sheets of rain hid it almost immediately. Back I went up the steep stairs where I was told to remove my shoes. I did. I waited for the hermit master and contemplated my damp belongings. All of this would need to be carried up to the high hermitage. I was a seacoast dweller. At 9000 feet I was already a little out of breath just sitting still.

Slow as a snail, time inched forward. I spent several hours of the afternoon in the kitchen drying off. Eyes on my briefcase, I thought about all the things I would work on in my solitude. How mistaken I was about that! At last the hermit master came. She was slight, a mother of three, with blue eyes and high cheekbones. In a cheerful and childlike voice she told me, "Take what you want from the larder. I'll carry the water." Not only my gear, but also all my provisions, would have to be walked up to the hermitage at 11,000 feet.

It was time to get provisions...into the rain I went again. I lifted the bulkhead of the larder, and the counterweight rose like a Calder sculpture on its rope. The cool ground served as the refrigerator. In the half light I gathered a few carrots, onions, zucchinis, brown rice, yogurt, and a loaf of bread...remembering every moment, that all of this had to be carried straight up and a long way. I passed on the cantaloupe and the acorn squash. They were too heavy.

Secretly, I was pleased to have brought coffee in my pack for there was none in the larder. The Lama Foundation was a vegetarian place. There were sprouts, granola, and ginseng tea, plus countless grains stored in big bins, but no coffee.

After another hour had gone by, the rain slacked off. I could still hear the pine needles dripping and smell the fresh scent of balsam. Wanting to get going, the hermit master stuffed the food in a well- used backpack. In each hand she held a gallon jug of water. She even offered to carry my briefcase. A little shame-faced, I accepted because I had my suitcase (turned backpack) on my shoulders. It easily weighed forty pounds. And then there was the bulky, unwieldy sleeping bag, not a tight sausage an experienced backpacker would carry. I held the bag in front of me like a huge baby and could barely see where I was going.

We were all ready to climb to the hermitage when we were interrupted by the whines of a child. The hermit master's little boy wanted his mother's attention. She told him to get his shoes on and to climb with us. He whined and wanted her to himself. She encouraged him to join us, and we walked him to the tent where they were living for the summer. Each prolonged moment the heavy backpack bit into my shoulders. Under my breath, I told myself to be patient, but there was not an ounce of it in my being. Instead, I noticed the chronic level of impatience I had...a kind of nervous system speed that insisted I get on with it...whatever *it* might be. I understood how persistently I always wanted to get on with things.

Finally, the suitcase became so heavy that I asked if I might go ahead. I knew the child would not be appeased without his mother's undivided attention any more than my nervous system could be appeased by patiently waiting. Relieved, I was given directions: *keep always to the left.*

A left-hand-path! "Aaah", I said to myself. The left-hand-path, the heart path, was the one that had always called me. But between action and simply being, I had almost always chosen action in the past. Would this change, I wondered, as I began to climb. In a few steps my breath became short. I had to stop. My heart was beating like a trapped bird in a cage. I felt dizzy. I took another few steps. Slowly I ascended, a mini step at a time, hugging the bulky Sears and Roebuck sleeping bag like an unwanted and awkward child, like the way I felt about myself. It took far more effort than I had imagined. With each step, sweat pearled and gathered on my upper lip, and I kept licking it off.

The red chunky bark of the ponderosa pines glistened from the rain. The wind in the trees sounded like rushing water. After an hour I had climbed up far enough to see the breathtaking view. Low clouds, streaked with gray and mauve, scudded over the plain. I was surrounded by beauty. Beauty above me. Beauty below me. Beauty to the right of me. Beauty to the left of me. The steep, stone-strewn trail before me. I was out of breath in every way.

After resting, I continued. Eventually, the roof of a strangely assembled hut came into sight. My chest was still heaving from the effort of climbing, but I moved towards the hut in anticipation. I knew I needed it for shelter. I needed it for solace and rest. I needed it for days of solitude.

Inside it was like most camps. It had a wood stove, one gas burner from a propane tank, a wooden bowl, one spoon, one knife, and one mattress in the window seat with a view into forever. It had two kerosene lamps, a meditation stool, toilet paper in a mouse-proof, plastic, ice cream container, some pots and pans, and silence. It seemed just right. I was glad to have arrived.

What a relief to shed the backpack, to roll out the sleeping bag, and to find a book of matches someone had picked up en route to this same destination. I knew I would need them. But the matchbook would become important in a way I wouldn't know until later. When the hermit master arrived with my briefcase and left the jugs of water, she told me that if I needed anything, I would just have to climb down and leave a note attached to the clothespin on the garbage can at the start of the trail. She said she would fill a day-pack for me any time. The thought of climbing down and up again was not something I gladly entertained. I decided then and there I would make do as long as possible. The hermit master left and silence began...rich, deep, and endless silence. It was what I had come for. As the stillness wrapped around me, I didn't know whether I felt comfort or fear. Perhaps it was a combination of both.

II

Blue...on Blue...
into Darker Blue

Slowly, I unpacked a few belongings and stowed my suitcase and briefcase in the rude closet with its leather strap for a door handle. I went outside and picked lupine, Indian paintbrush, and a yellow flower whose name I didn't know. An empty coffee can served as a vase. I wanted the bouquet to remind me I was at home, though I was far from feeling it yet. Lastly, I unpacked the black prayer bowl made at the Santa Clara Pueblo. Its round emptiness had invited me to purchase it. Would it be a symbol for me here in the hermitage...an invitation to just be?

Outside the entrance to the hut was a trail into the woods. I thought it might lead to an outhouse. Indeed, it was an outhouse, but without walls. There was a wooden seat in the open, no roof or walls, but a spectacular view. It made me smile. Toilet paper would have to be brought for every trip. Suddenly, I remembered the outhouse above the Arctic Circle from my childhood. Unlike the one before me, that outhouse had a roof and wonderful cartoons hanging on the walls. I deeply appreciated what seemed to be a weaving from the past to the present, happening as I stood there. Being here in the Sangre de Christo Mountains was certainly a link to my earlier camp experiences. But older than that, were warm memories of the mountains in Sweden. Recognition shivered up my spine and I felt a sense of peace.

By then it was supper time. On the one burner I concocted a soupy, gooey mess of rice and vegetables. Finding an old jar of cayenne and some spices, I sprinkled the concoction liberally with them. Begging bowl in hand, I sat on the window seat that cantilevered out from the hut and took my first meal in the hermitage.

After dinner, I leisurely cleaned up. The silence grew deeper. Light began to fall. The distant landscape turned blue in every shade imaginable. I watched the colors shift and move...blue... on blue...into darker blue. I felt an old sadness well up. I was here to know this, to witness it, not avoiding but joining what I saw outside with what I felt inside...blue...on blue...on blue and darkness.

An inner, practical voice told me, *You're tired. Go to sleep.* I brushed my teeth outside in the night. Then, by a single candle's light, I curled up in the brown and russet, Sears and Roebuck special. After blowing out the flame and tucking a pillow under my head, I let the night take over. Everything felt strange, most especially that there was no ambient light. Close to my head, I heard a mouse scratching in the wall. There was nothing I could do but accept that I was sharing the hut with other creatures who knew it as home. I mused that the word *ear* was embedded in the word hear, and that I had no ear lids to protect me from the sounds around me. As I listened to the scratching, I knew I was meant to hear every little thing in the hut and outside its walls as well. The last sound before I fell asleep was a large housefly buzzing against the windowpane above me in the sleeping alcove.

III

Once More...Joy!

Five a.m. I sat up with a jerk. Intense morning light poured in. For a moment I was disoriented, and then I realized where I was. Here. Here. Here, alone in silence for many days. It felt scary. So I reassured myself and said, *Today I will write and read and meditate and hike and draw and...* Mobilized with high intentions, I brewed coffee and took it outside where there was a stump by the doorstep waiting for me.

A cup of coffee later I was back in the hut gazing out from the sleeping alcove to the splendor beyond it. The landscape unrolled, huge and generous. My shoulders relaxed. My eyes could barely take in the beauty before me. Here were miles and miles of mesas and rugged gorges dotted with low mesquite bushes and pines. The Rio Grande Valley spread out into forever. I was reduced to the right size again: so very tiny in vastness. It was a good feeling, and one I remembered having had long ago on my first visit to New Mexico.

Eyes still in a daze, my hand brushed against something on top of the sleeping bag. It was the red book of matches I had used the night before to light my candle. Now I could read what it said on the cover: *Royal Guest* was printed in bold letters. I smiled. It was true that I was a guest here, and I wondered how many had stayed in this hut on the edge of nowhere and everywhere? I could feel there had been many...all royal guests. I sensed how, not only here, but also everywhere, in life itself, we are royal guests. It was a clear message that I tucked inside of me to take home and remember.

The days flowed into one another. I didn't write or draw or hike much further than the outhouse. The land took me into its arms, and it was as if I had disappeared into it. Almost every afternoon it rained hard. And then came the rainbows arching over the plains. Sometimes there were two or three. The pines around the hut glistened with water droplets. The light kept shifting, and the vast valley changed color from dun to rust to mauve.

I put out pots and pans to catch rainwater. I didn't want to budge and have to climb down that steep trail for water or provisions. A natural fast began, and the deep bodily quiet that goes with fasting descended. My friend, Lee, was not with me, but I felt I had his brotherly presence within me.

Slowly my mind quieted, and my need to perform left me. My body relaxed. I felt more open, and I could feel that my usual self-protective tendencies had left me. On the fourth day, as I sat outside by the doorway on the stump that was there, I heard the *whirr* of wings. As if from another time and place, a hummingbird came close. From the moment I first heard those wings, I kept as still as I could. The bird hovered before me, gazing with its small, jet black eyes into mine. The wings moved so fast they were a blur. Here was my living image of joy...alive and back again...as a visitation and confirmation I recognized. Inside, I knew I had two wings, too, and that I whirred with joy. The veil was thin once more.

IV

In a Field of Lupines

Days merged into one another. Writing and reading did not happen. Suitcase and briefcase stayed in the closet. I wore the same clothes day in and day out and washed out my underwear daily. I brushed my teeth on the hill under the stars. When I was thirsty, I drank rainwater from the black prayer bowl. And I slept and slept.

Every notion of having to do something disappeared. The days filled with simple *being*. It was enough to watch chipmunks feed as they delicately bent the grass heads full of seed. The intimate feel of silence hugged me. From time to time I cried, allowing deep, unspoken hurts, longings, and confusions to rise up from inner places not unlike the clouds that rose from the vast valley below. So much was showering free in those afternoon rains. Much of it I couldn't name. But I could feel an old heaviness leave me. In the space that opened, I found an immense sense of gratitude.

On the last day of my stay, I took a short walk into the forest. I found deer droppings and bear scat. For me, animal friends from long ago were not gone. Though they were invisible, I could feel they were close. The afternoon rain had passed. Rainbows arched over the mesas. Sitting on the stump outside of the door listening to the dripping from the trees, I saw a doe emerge from under the pines. She was only a stone's throw from me, so close. But I felt she was here from long ago. She wiggled her ears. She gazed at me a long time deciding whether she could trust me. She waited. I waited, sitting very still. Then it seemed that she felt I was a safe one. Slowly, she pushed two fawns forward into the clearing in front of the hut. Standing there behind them, she showed them off, clearly saying, *Aren't they marvelous?* I recognized mother-pride, having felt it often in my time, too. Yes, they were marvelous, and this was a sacred moment. I nodded my head in acknowledgment. She wiggled her ears, snorted and slowly melted back into the trees again. I felt how strands from many parts of my life wound together into a simple wholeness.

The last afternoon at the hermitage, I sat high up on the hill behind the hut in a field of lupines. I wanted to say goodbye. I wanted to say thank you to the land, the vastness, and the silence. I wondered how I was going to nurture and preserve what I had experienced here at the high hermitage and with my friend, Lee. My life in the world was busy and full of people. I loved that. I also loved how, in silence and in nature, other worlds opened and touched me deeply. Could I bring together these two ways of being in the world?

Suddenly there was no silence on the hill. From everywhere came the sound of humming. The bees descended. Every other flower had a bee. Inches from my legs the lupine rose, purple and blue, and the bees were in the flower heads humming and feeding. It was a rich and happy sound, the sound of action and being as one! The bees were doing what they needed to do. I knew as they did so, they were also pollinating flowers for another season of continued growth.

The sound penetrated me. It was the sound of being fully alive. I knew it would go home with me. I would try to live my authentic self and let my actions flow from that center of being. I realized that whenever any of us are true to our essence and do what belongs to us to do, we serve *Life*. Then, like bees, we will be inadvertent pollinators as well, and so help others to grow. I also knew I would trust that the veil is always thin, though we might not recognize or understand it.

When we are good for each other there is mutual radiance everywhere, be it with creatures or humans. Fully present in the here and in the now, we are all royal guests on this planet.

Telling Your Story

After Thoughts

Thank you for reading these stories. They happened long ago, but they are as fresh inside me today as when they happened. Metaphysically, we can be sure that what we keep returning to in thought tends to manifest in reality. That makes it important to know what our souls yearn for and to be careful about serving the life that can be found in our deep longings. It is also important to own our blessings and to tell others about them. The telling helps us integrate those meaningful events that nurtured our souls.

Even if no one else is listening, it's important to tell *yourself* your heart-full stories. They will be heard and received in some unknown and mysterious ways, for nothing falls out of reality. To name in gratitude those persons who most helped us become the one we are is a reverent act. To reflect on the specifics of how they enhanced our growth will reverberate in our being. It is good to be nourished again by the depth of those gifts. How good they were for us. How good we were for them.

When we can find even a little gratitude toward those persons who made our lives difficult, and were therefore catalysts for our growth, we mend our inner world. Blessing those persons takes away the sting of power we felt they had over us. We establish our own place to stand and be. We can always breathe more tenderly as lovers of all beings. Our wounds then become portals into more wholeness and new ways of living.

To recognize and write down the mutuality that already exists in our lives will also help us consider where we might give more of ourselves.

A sense of being *called*, and wanting to engage in that call, is a sure and trustworthy sign of the true adventures in life that belong to us. Our blessing minds can notice, partake in, and support the inherent goodness all around us, despite the fearful conditions we see that are very real, and have arisen from our collective fears. Blessing is social activism on a cellular level. It is available to everyone.

There will never be anyone just like us ever again. In this moment we are already blessings. Spirit does not take its gifts back. The African saying, "*I am because we are*", is a profound truth. To live with such awareness is to be fully human. It allows a life of mutuality. As the Quaker saying goes, it is allowing "*that of God*" in each of us, to shine and to act. Every one of us is needed in the serving of *Life*. We are each part of a profound, evolving, and radiant whole.

About the Author

Gunilla Norris, a psychotherapist in private practice for forty years, has had the privilege of accompanying many people on their journeys to growth and healing. Her has taught meditation and led contemplative workshops of many kinds. She has published eleven children's books, two books of poetry and ten books on spirituality including: *Being Home*, *Becoming Bread*, *Inviting Silence*, *Embracing the Seasons*, *A Mystic Garden*, *Simple Ways*, *Match*, *Sheltered in the Heart*, *Companions on the Way*, and *Great Love in Little Ways*.

WWW.GUNILLANORRIS.COM

LITTLE
BOUND BOOKS

OTHER OFFERINGS TO CONSIDER

WWW.LITTLEBOUNDBOOKS.COM

LOOK FOR OUR TITLES WHEREVER BOOKS ARE SOLD